Valerie Duncan

Crickets in My Lunchbox?

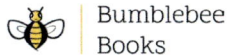

BUMBLEBEE PAPERBACK EDITION

Copyright © Valerie Duncan 2024

The right of Valerie Duncan to be identified as author of
this work has been asserted in accordance with sections
77 and 78 of the Copyright, Designs and Patents Act 1988.

All Rights Reserved

No reproduction, copy or transmission of this publication
may be made without written permission.
No paragraph of this publication may be reproduced,
copied or transmitted save with the written permission of the publisher,
or in accordance with the provisions
of the Copyright Act 1956 (as amended).

Any person who commits any unauthorised act in relation to
this publication may be liable to criminal
prosecution and civil claims for damage.

A CIP catalogue record for this title is
available from the British Library.

ISBN: 978-1-78796-024-4

*Bumblebee Books is an imprint of
Olympia Publishers.*

First Published in 2024

**Bumblebee Books
Tallis House
2 Tallis Street
London
EC4Y 0AB**

Printed in Great Britain

www.olympiapublishers.com

Acknowledgements

I must start by thanking Owen Davey and the House of Illustration for setting me on the path to illustrating non-fiction books for children. To the Edinburgh Children's Illustrators, thank you for the fun, laughter and your words of wisdom. Finally, thank you to my mother and my great friends Anne and Vivienne for their support and encouragement and for listening to me going on about my illustration projects for many years!

Contents

7. Entomophagy, what's that?

9. It's not so unusual.

10. It's a tradition.

12. All sorts of snacks

14. Taste test

16. Popularity contest

18. Yuck reaction

 20. Hidden in plain sight.

 22. A new way to eat.

 24. They are good for you.

 26. Chef's table

 28. Greenhouse effect

 30. Farming revolution

 32. So what have we learned?

Entomophagy, what's that?

In the Western World, people don't generally eat insects. However, over 2 billion people around the world do eat insects every day. People have been eating insects as long as they have walked on the Earth. Having a diet of insects is called entomophagy. There are almost 2,000 edible insect species around the world.

It's not so unusual.

Africa has the biggest range of edible insects. There are more than 500 different edible insect species living in Africa so unsurprisingly insect eating is more common in Africa than anywhere else in the world.

It's a tradition.

There are lots of examples of people around the world enjoying insects.

In the markets in Mexico, they sell piles of roasted chapulines (grasshoppers).

In Indonesia, people dip a reed in palm sap and wave it in the air to catch dragonflies to boil or fry.

Native Americans roasted June bugs over coals and ate them like popcorn.

Emperor Hirohito of Japan liked
boiled wasps with rice.

In Papua New Guinea the walking stick insect
is eaten and its legs are used as fish-hooks.

All sorts of snacks

Many insects are highly nutritious and they each taste different.

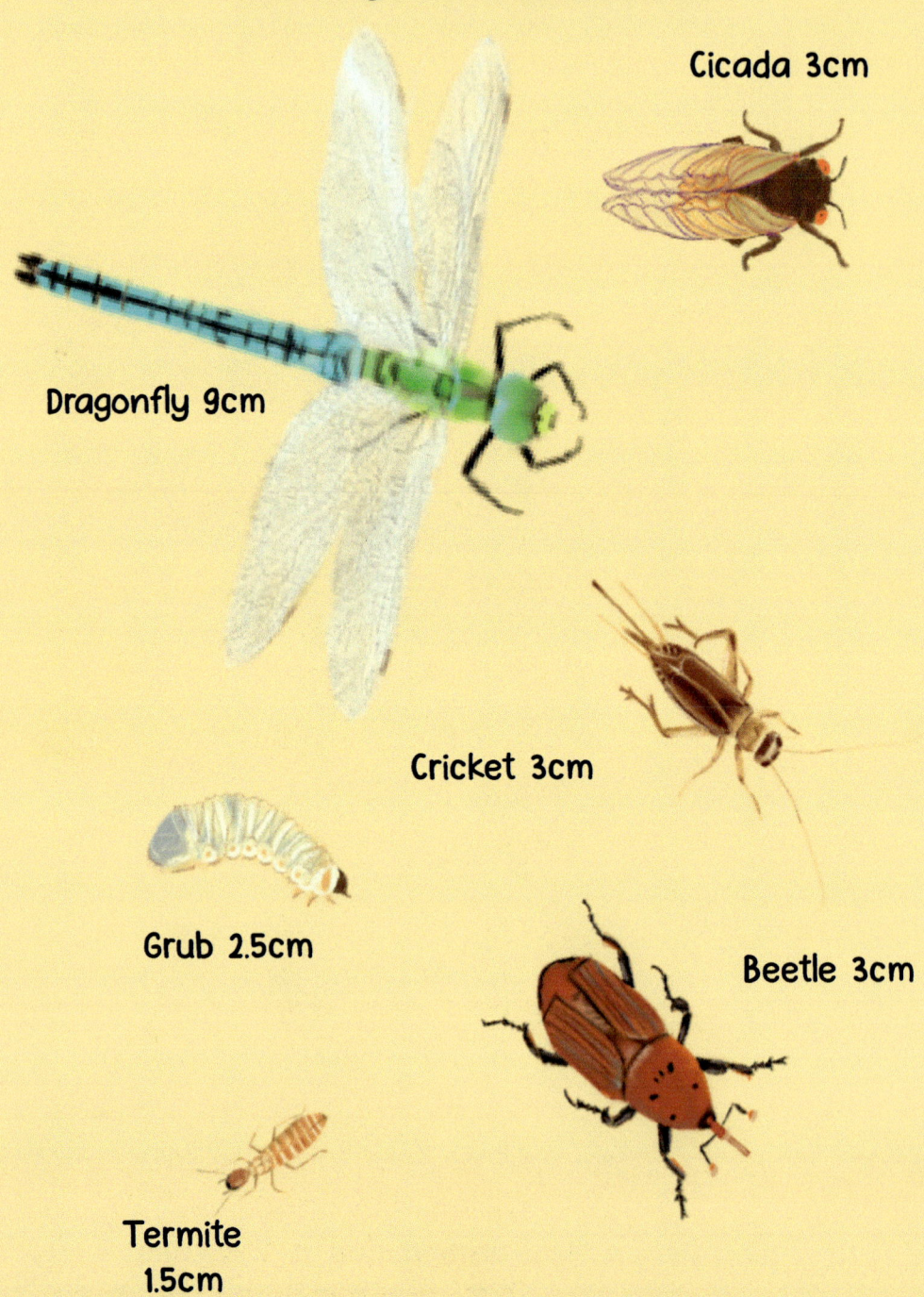

Cicada 3cm

Dragonfly 9cm

Cricket 3cm

Grub 2.5cm

Beetle 3cm

Termite 1.5cm

Taste test
What do insects taste like?

It can be difficult to imagine and describe what insects taste like and people might describe the taste of each type of insect differently but most generally agree that:

Cockroaches taste like mushrooms.

Raw termites taste like pineapple.

Fried grasshoppers taste like sardines.

Crickets taste like popcorn.

Popularity contest

Globally, the most eaten insects by humans are -

17% Caterpillars

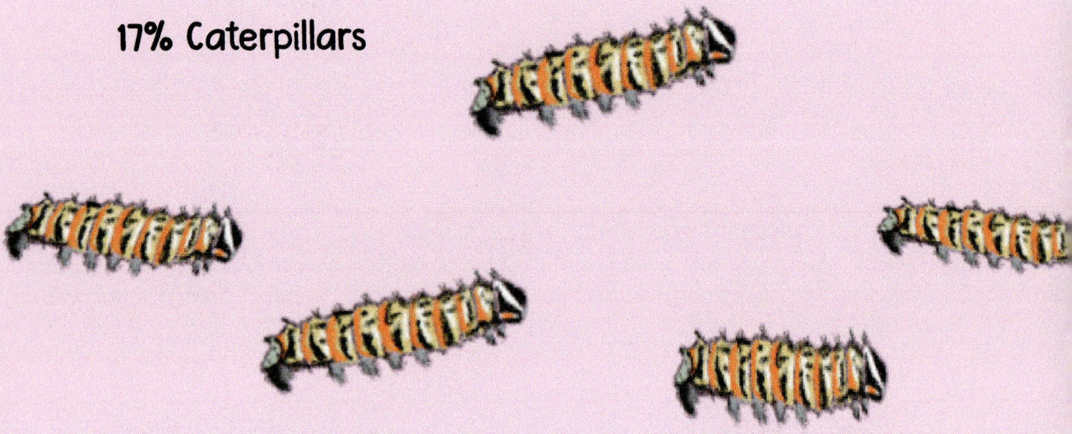

14% Grasshoppers, locusts and crickets

31% Beetles

15% Bees, wasps and ants

11% Cicadas, leaf hoppers and scale insects

9% Dragonflies

3% Termites

Yuck reaction

Your "Yuck" reaction is all in your head.
As young children we are taught to be careful:
Wasps will sting us.
Flies carry diseases.
Beetles can bite.
Bees might sting.

Your body is trying to keep you safe. It keeps us "creeped out" about insects so we stay away from danger.

But many insects are not harmful to us and if you had been eating insects all your life you wouldn't think twice about enjoying them.

Hidden in plain sight.

Don't like the idea of eating insects?
You already eat insects, but you don't realise it.

It turns out we eat around 450 - 900 grams of insects per year. There are small parts of insects in many foods. Many flavour and colour additives come from insects.

Cochineal

One of the most commonly used colours is cochineal. Cochineal is a tiny, cactus-dwelling insect that makes a glorious red colour. You might find it is used to colour strawberry ice cream. Don't worry bugs are generally safer to eat than the artificial colours that are used in food as an alternative.

Kerria Lacca

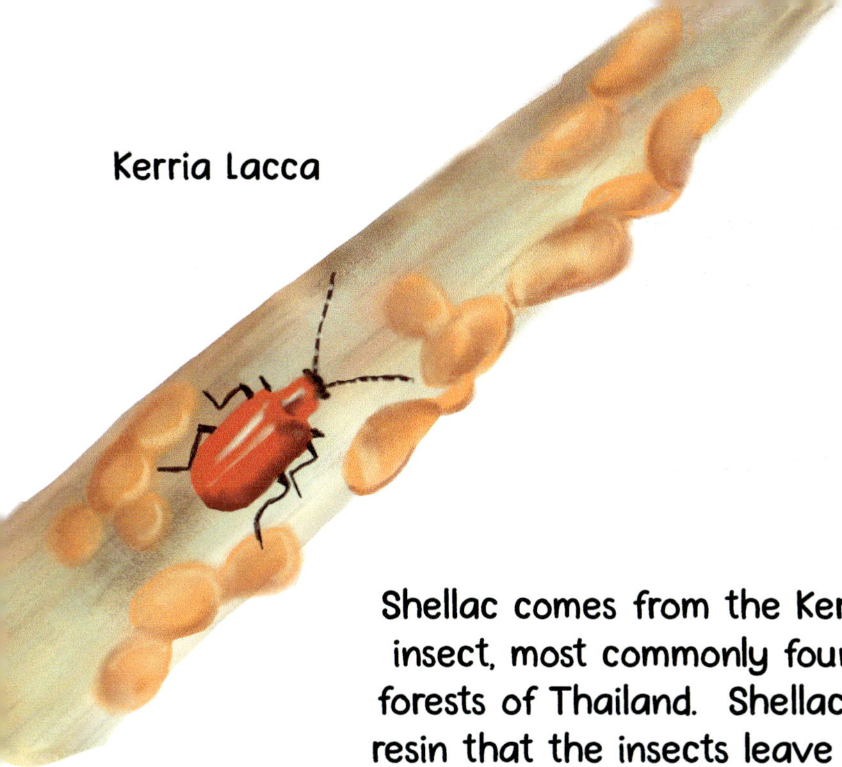

Shellac comes from the Kerria Lacca insect, most commonly found in the forests of Thailand. Shellac is a hard resin that the insects leave behind on trees. It is used to coat sweets like Jelly Beans to make them shiny.

Honeybees

Honey has been swallowed and spat out hundreds of times by honeybees before we collect and enjoy it.

A new way to eat.

The time has come to find new answers to the problem of climate change and the impact it is having on food shortages around the world.

EAT MORE INSECTS!

The Food and Agriculture Organisation of the United Nations is encouraging more entomophagy to help address this problem as insects are a more efficient food source.

Let's compare - 88% of an insect is edible (the only parts that should be removed in most cases are the legs and wings), but only 40% of pork and beef is edible.

They are good for you.

Everyone needs to eat a balanced diet to stay healthy. Edible insects contain high-quality protein, vitamins, minerals and amino acids. Some insects have at least the same if not higher nutritional value than the meats we commonly eat like beef and chicken.

Nutritional information for 100g ground beef and grasshopper.

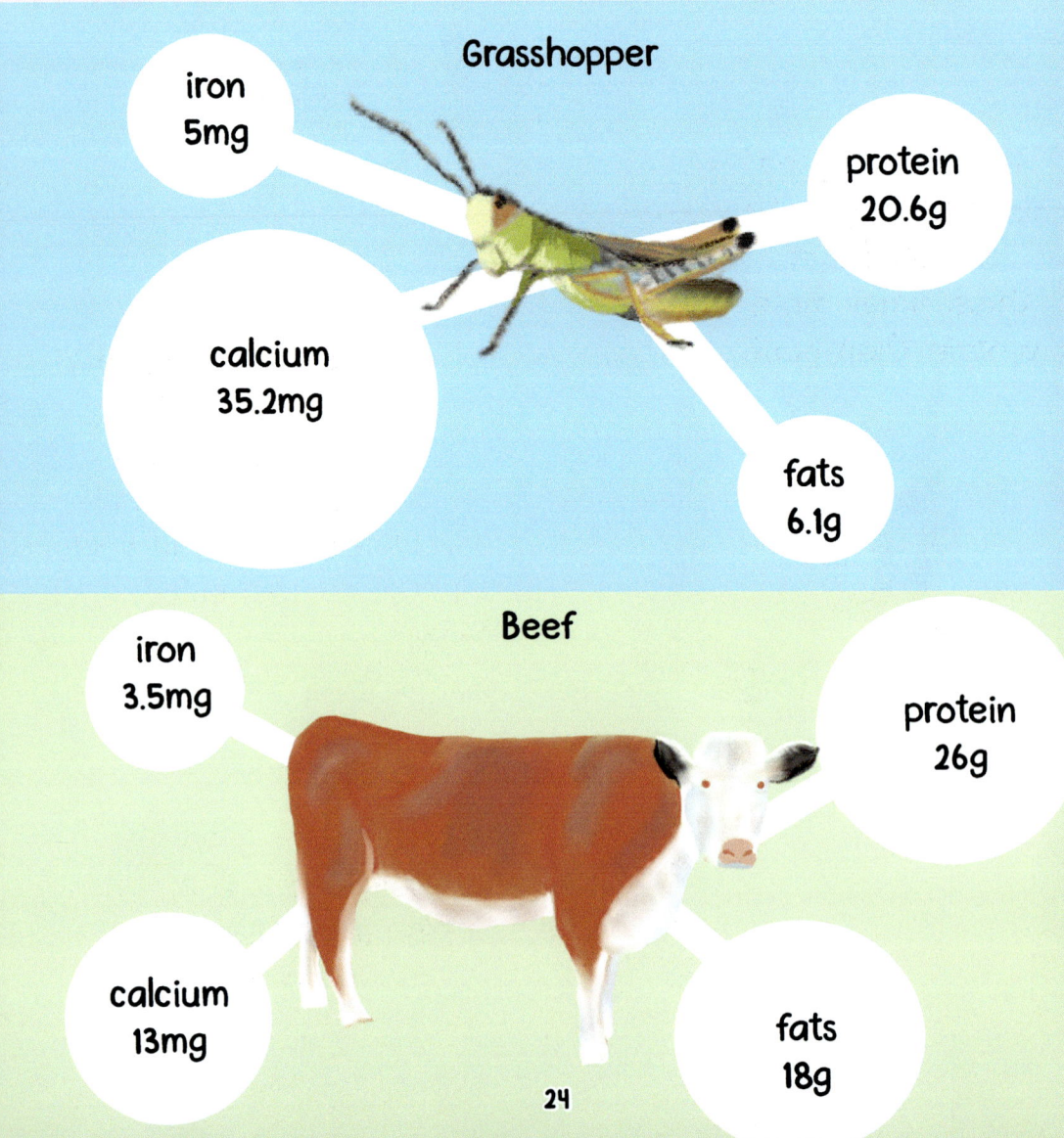

Grasshopper
- iron 5mg
- protein 20.6g
- calcium 35.2mg
- fats 6.1g

Beef
- iron 3.5mg
- protein 26g
- calcium 13mg
- fats 18g

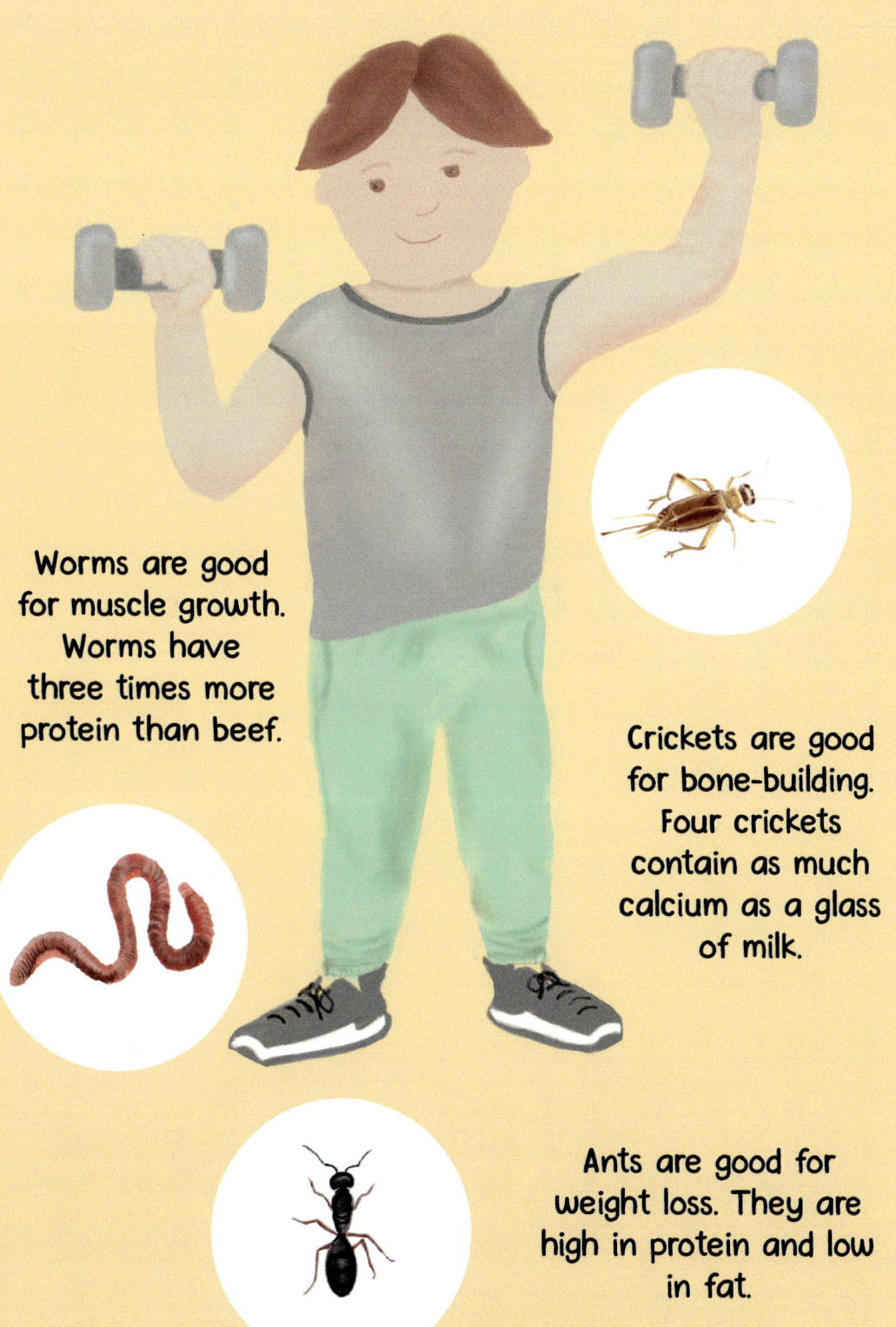

Chef's table

You can make lots of different foods from insects. You don't have to eat them whole.

Crickets are made into flour that can then be used to make bread, pasta and cakes.

Chopped up and pureed mealworms are made into burgers, crisps and protein bars.

Entomilk is created by blending the larvae of the black soldier fly. This diary-free milk alternative can then be turned into ice cream in all sorts of flavours from chocolate to peanut butter.

Greenhouse effect

Greenhouse gases are one of the causes of climate change. The largest chunk of food-related greenhouse gases comes from farming. This is about 18% of all global greenhouse gases. This includes:
- Methane (CH_4) from cattle's digestive process.
- Nitrous oxide (N_2O) from fertilisers for crop production.
- Carbon dioxide (CO_2) from cutting down forests for the expansion of farmland.

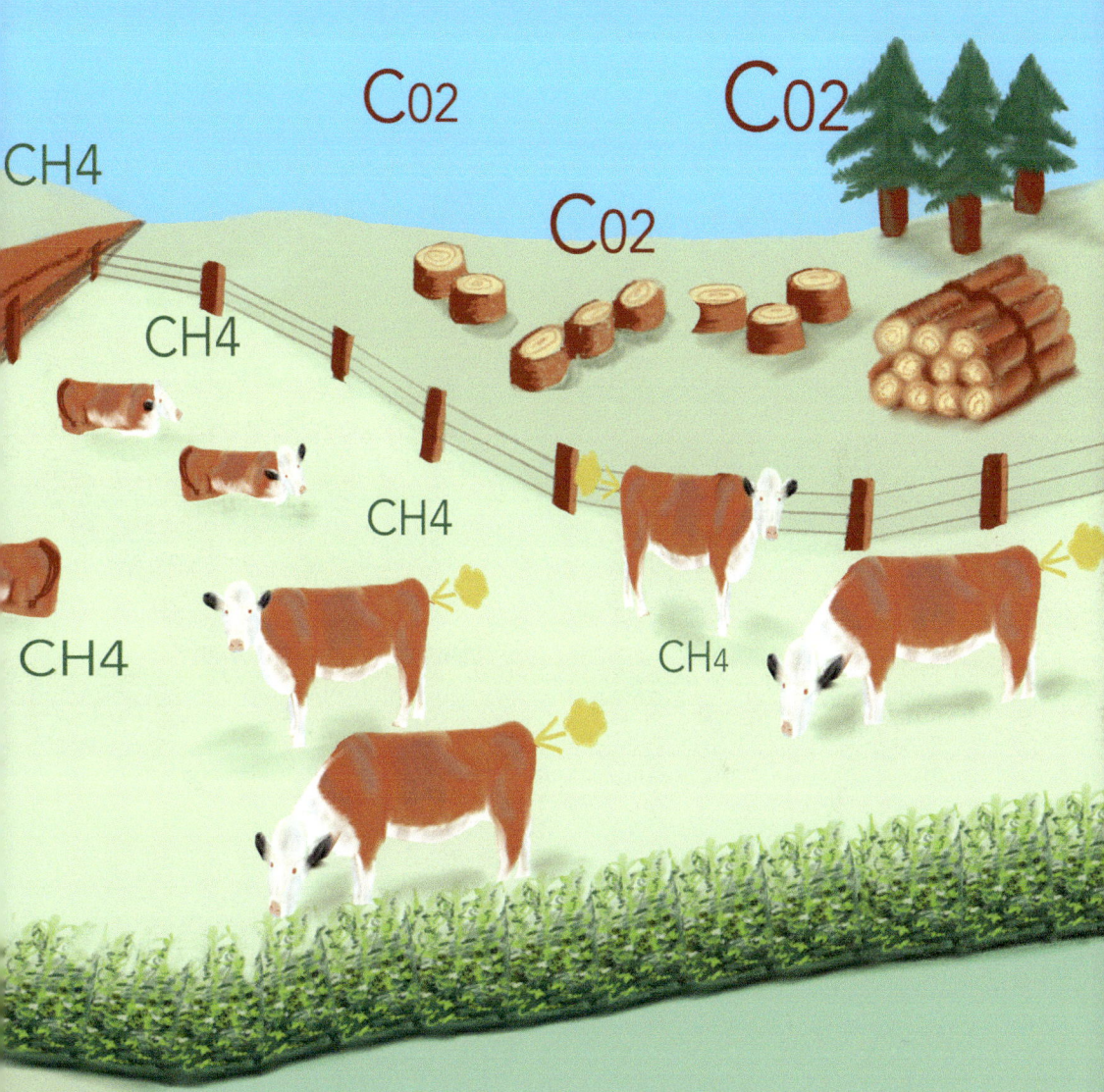

Edible insects can be more environmentally friendly than traditional farm animals. They emit fewer greenhouse gases and ammonia and can be fed on organic waste.

Farming revolution

Most edible insects are harvested from the wild.

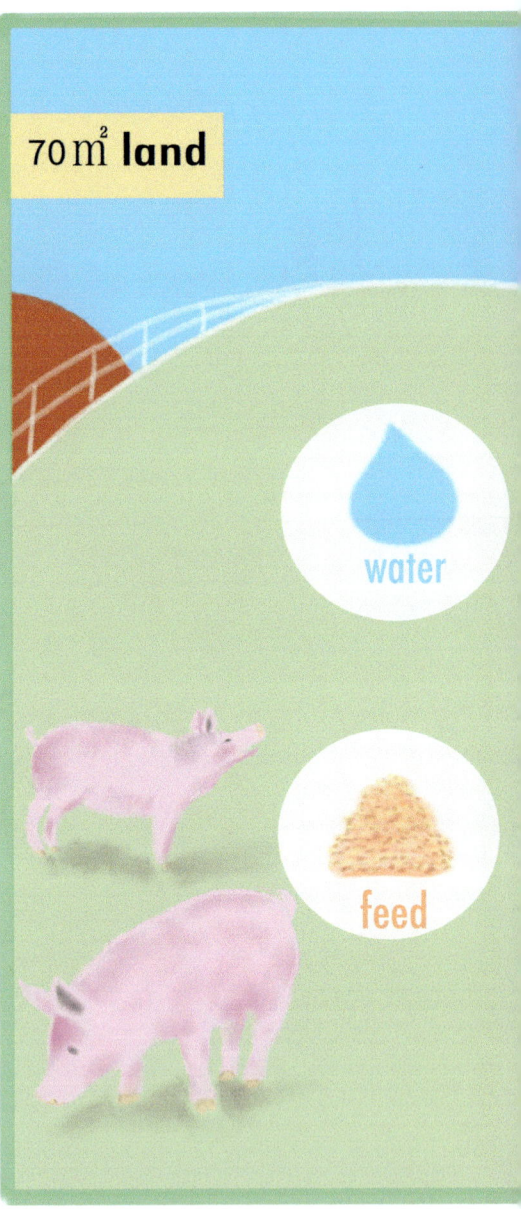

The amount of land, water and feed needed to produce 1kg of protein from beef.

The amount of land, water and feed needed to produce 1kg of protein from pork.

Insects are good to farm because they don't need a lot of space and produce protein quickly.

The amount of land, water and feed needed to produce 1kg of protein from chicken.

The amount of land, water and feed needed to produce 1kg of protein from crickets.

So, what have we learned?

Insects take up little space to breed - Crates of edible insects such as crickets can be stacked on top of each other like bug apartments.

A lot of the world's population already eat edible insects. They taste delicious and are versatile.

By eating insects one day per week, you would save over 100,000 litres of water per year.

They don't have to look like bugs when you eat them. When bugs are made into flour you can't even see them.

The protein in bugs can help keep us strong and healthy.

About the Author

Crickets in My Lunchbox? is written and illustrated by Valerie Duncan. Valerie has lived in the beautiful rural and coastal area of East Lothian most of her life. She enjoys drawing and painting animals and nature. The view from her studio window looks across the fields towards North Berwick Law and provides plenty of inspiration. Valerie is an experienced Primary School teacher, who is aware of the importance of the impact of climate change on the future of the children she teaches. *Crickets in My Lunchbox?* is Valerie's first children's non-fiction book.